MW01251357

giacometti's girl

poems by sandra davies

Cormorant Books

Copyright © 2018 Sandra Davies
This edition copyright © 2018 Cormorant Books Inc.
This is a first edition.

No part of this publication may be reproduced, stored in a retrieval system
or transmitted, in any form or by any means, without the prior written consent
of the publisher or a licence from The Canadian Copyright Licensing Agency
(Access Copyright). For an Access Copyright licence,
visit www.accesscopyright.ca or call toll free 1.800.893.5777.

The publisher gratefully acknowledges the support of the Canada Council for the
Arts and the Ontario Arts Council for its publishing program. We acknowledge
the financial support of the Government of Canada through the Canada Book
Fund (CBF) for our publishing activities, and the Government of Ontario through
the Ontario Media Development Corporation, an agency of the Ontario Ministry
of Culture, and the Ontario Book Publishing Tax Credit Program.

LIBRARY AND ARCHIVES CANADA CATALOGUING IN PUBLICATION

Davies, Sandra, 1940–, author
Giacometti's girl / Sandra Davies.

Poems.
ISBN 978-1-77086-541-9 (softcover)

I. Title.

PS8607.A95255G53 2018   C811'.6   C2018-903813-6

Cover design: angeljohnguerra.com
Interior text design: Tannice Goddard, bookstopress.com
Printer: Sunville Printco

Printed and bound in Canada.

CORMORANT BOOKS INC.
260 SPADINA AVENUE, SUITE 502, TORONTO, ON M5T 2E4
www.cormorantbooks.com

for Shelagh who started it all
for Nathalie who read every poem
for my family
and
in loving memory of
my brother Tim, poet

Contents

giacometti's girl

House Wren

A flick of the tiny up-tilted head before she hollers
her best good night into the evening sky. From high above,
under the curve of the world's ceiling, I must seem
as insignificant to her as she is miniscule to me.
She doesn't give me a glance,

this rackety bird, unobtrusive in her smooth
dun-colour, its underlay of peach when the light is right:
compact, no bigger than a deer mouse, with a voice
persistent and scrappy as a terrier's.
She shows up every May,

occupies the wren house, sweet, brave, hilarious,
closer to my heart than I have understood —
hatches babies, scolds, protects. Then exits.
One morning, just before dawn, I catch her poking
around the deck. Quiet. Oblivious.

Sometimes, in a piece by Mozart, you can hear
a perfectly measured, exquisite run of slow true
notes. They come to me, from time to time,
like prayer, like heartbreak, like a tough little
wren on a deck in the woods by herself.

Giacometti's Girl

Facing squarely front,
head erect, hands folded,
a young woman sits very still
staring out into the world —

I got her at the Tate a lifetime ago.
Or perhaps, she got me,
reached out with her sober gaze
and looked me in the eye —
so compelling, this Giacometti study,
one of a series of this girl.

She is waiting,
waiting to meet the one,
waiting to open, to lie down,

waiting for him to come home,
for the baby to quicken,
for birth, growth,
laughing, loving, leaving,

and for everything else along the way,
betrayal, loss,
the hungry waves of the sea.

Even then in that gallery
when I was young I must
have understood

how we women sit braced, contained,
hearts willed to steady,
waiting with guarded eyes
for God's other shoe.

Beppe Speaks

I waited always for the knock. We women had to answer and we slept with pistols under our pillows — rifles were hard to get and were carried only by the men. Motherhood came second, you see, our babies weaned on boiled turnip, left with *tantes* who filled them up with more turnip, *omkes* who carved them toys from turnip. Our men were fighters, but we were only couriers, and had to be the first to sacrifice. We could not question my husband Hendrick who was *kommandant* of our group.

Once we had to get the hidden Jewish *kinderen* off the houseboat where we lived — move them to a safer place — and Hendrick hid them under blankets in the truck. He had to shoot the German officer who tried to stop them but he never told me this until we came to Canada. To tell you true I think he thought that Jesus wouldn't save him from hell if he knew he had killed a man. (So often you remember he prayed the *Onze Vader*). Another time there was a drop — you know a "drop"? An army plane — food supplies, guns, soldiers. We all ran to the airfield with the flares. And there was silence on the ground and silence from the soldiers, no stars or moon is why they chose that night. That silence — flares and parachutes, the smell of fear, and I thought about my baby, my empty breasts. Running fast and low we carried everything, soldiers, guns, food, ghosts. They came so silently, those German gunboats — how they slipped unseen into the canal to hunt us down we did not know. We ran the motor, stole away, we lived. I see me now, a girl of twenty, riding on my bicycle, carrying documents, carrying a pistol — for Christiaan, for my baby boy. That he should live in peace.

Remembrance Day

All tidied up for us, no sense of cold wet
trenches, sucking mud, the constant
crack of guns — these crosses row on row
bring memories of my grandfather,
shell-shocked, and of me, the grandgirl
held captive by his ceaseless grimacing,
the mask of deep despair, a chaos of mind
I could not then name.

Under a dull aluminum sky, in this cold
eleventh month of stinging rain,
rotting leaves, muck — I think of him today.
The way he sat me on his lap, offered
his twisted smile. The way his white hair
stood out like a cloud. His bony knees.

A Paradox

Mother of my mother. Housedress limp
from too many washings, she would turn to me,
flushed from marathon baking,
wipe doughy scraps from her hands
in one deft downward swoop,
then flour-up again, knead and pummel,
one ear open to my small-girl fantasies,
triumphs and woes.

Leaning in, strong arms readying our
daily bread, she would listen, cluck,
murmur from her endless cache of
love sounds. Effortless comfort dependable
as breath. A balm for every season.
She spoiled me. Everybody knew.

What I knew was that my mother seethed.
She never even bothered with her own,
my mother said. *Never even liked us.*

Oxford Street

Before their wedding, he takes her to the market
in the old neighbourhood,
fading brick houses, worn *mezuzahs*
nailed beside the entranceways.

To Oxford Street where he was born,
where his mother wouldn't let him cross
the street till he was ten, where he watched
his older brother sprint with friends
to noisy dirty pool halls when they should
have been in school. *Meshugeners*!

They gorge on noodle kugel, garlicked brisket,
sugared cheese buns, watch the *shochet*
slaughter chickens in his bloody shop
among the clamouring Russian, Polish, Yiddish
of prewar immigrants, those who got out
in time to mourn the ones who didn't.

Oh, the Friday scent of baking challah, roasting meat;
the old black-clad bubbies who knew she wasn't one of them.
On a morning visit to the crumbling synagogue
she watches, long hair covered,
peers through tiny windows at a *minyan* of
elders in prayer shawls, bowing, nodding,
davening, she knows it's called.

They were young. Too innocent to foresee
perils in such a marriage. But fifty years of absence
have somehow kept the old *shul*
full of light for her, the yearning ever fresh
for those fragrant warm embraces.
For those women, their stories,
their holding on to life.
Their belonging.

The Cure

Shy Uncle Leo, mother's youngest brother,
struggled and stuttered his way through life,
wrenching his wet face this way and that,
furious, helpless, never having his say.

T's were by far the hardest. Terrible tutting
T's erupting from his twisting, tortured tongue.
Catastrophic C's. A desperation of D's.
Wading through the wuh's was unwatchable.

We hated to see him coming, crossed streets
to avoid him, held tight to our embarrassment,
becoming at once villains, monsters of unfeeling,
running fast from what we couldn't fix.

Then he learned to sing — my mother
taught him — read it in a healer's book.
Music ended wordlessness. He caroled out his sentences,
secured a job delivering groceries for Costello's.

Suddenly the back stoops and front verandahs
of nondescript old Guilford Street
were laced with arias for asparagus,
hymns to horse-radish, bruised-banana blues.

Without a Script

1. December 25, 2003

There is no way to fix this.

My mother is ninety-six,
lives in a facility,
genteel, Catholic;
caregivers who often
really care.

I put her there some months ago
when she fell and broke her hip.

She's killed me off —
thinks I'm dead,
weeps for me
from time to time,
but mostly lashes out.

Or sits silent. Lost
in her wheelchair,
she doesn't know
it's Christmas.
Or that I miss her.

2. Holding

Four in the morning
phone shrills me awake —
mother —
I must go —

Stars, highway empty
except for a sixteen wheeler,
headlights bearing down
then gone.

Security guard waits.
He knows I'm coming,
he's used to this,
doesn't meet my eyes.

Night sister talks and talks
(shut *up*!) of fever, vomiting,
pneumonia — But she is kind,
and I have manners,
and say thank you.

Old human soul in the bed
doesn't know me.
She's ripped her clothes off.
My eyes recoil
from the diapered skeleton,
frail chest dragging for air,
gnarled feet.
Rest now.
I'm here, I'm here,
over and over —

I hold her like a child,
taut skin burning
from fires within.
But when I reach
for her fingers
their coolness shocks,
and in her absence
I bring them gently
to my forehead.

3. Trying

They've dressed her
neat and clean
in a new nightgown
I had made for her.
She beams at us,
How do I look in purple?
The nurses laugh,
happy to see her smiling for a change.

Hold me, she says —
I do, not knowing
if she recognizes this remaining child,
the one who didn't die,
the one with whom she's called a truce,
the daughter who looks after her.

I visit every day,
offer her tea,
try to feed her
but she'll have none of it.
I sit. I watch.

Do what you can for me.
I know she understands
she's dying, even
enjoying it somewhat,
the drama — we're more alike
than either of us cares to say.

Every day
I tell her that I love her
but I'm not sure.
Whether I can do it, I mean.
Every day.

4. Failing

Today I want her to disappear.

She is so old.
She has almost died
so many times.
Today I weep,
sure she is giving in
after the heart failings,
the broken hip,
dementia cracking the
elegant-lady veneer
exposing the soft body,
its animal needs,
infant squall.

But no —
spitting and scratching,
lost to me again,
she hangs on.
I need to grieve for her,
for the mother of my childhood.
And I want this nasty witch
to go away.

5. Wondering

She's still
in this world.
But going somewhere.
Hasn't eaten in two weeks.
She's drinking fluids, say the nurses,
but we can't force her, you know.
As if I'd want them to.

I don't come here every day now
and they look at me.
I don't know what they think
but I feel guilty.
Maybe they don't think anything.
Maybe I bestow this judgment
all by myself.

We have said our piece,
my mother and I,
voiced the proper words,
the expected phrases.
We've had such struggles
that it's hard to know
what constitutes our truth.
How can I please her?
How does she want this to unfold?
Politely, with lots of quiet tears?
Or with a wolf-howl.

6. Feeling

She's asleep this time.
I sit and watch.
I'm desperate for truth,
but the old rage licks
around my heart.
Better keep the lid on,
best to feel nothing.
Pain gauge on empty.

Suddenly she screams,
mouth open like a baby bird,
pointy red tongue protruding,
terror everywhere.
My back, my back,
over and over,
and then in French,
Le dos, le dos, le dos!

I'm afraid to touch her
but I do. I hold her
and she knows it's me.
Says it's good. Breathes in
and out. Whispers in my ear.
I'm afraid, she says.
Of what? of what?
(I'll not feel nothing now.
I'm going to fix this.
There will be love.)

Of *screaming*, she says.
I can't help it.
My tears fall and fall.

7. Noticing

Beautiful today
sitting in the wheelchair,
her white hair a nimbus,
this impossibly tiny woman
in her flowered dress,
ancient skin pulled tight and smooth,
hawk nose, carved bones
no longer hidden under
smooth, plump flesh.

My lovely mother —
sculpted by whichever god
sees to the dying,
a gift for those of us
who live.
She tells me she is very old,
has *trouble* in her back,
opens a perfect round mouth
for the pain pill,
makes no distinction
between daughter and nurse,
closes her eyes.
I notice her eyelids are transparent,
her lashes silver.

8. Remembering

Your husband died
twenty years ago
Mama, remember?
I brought you flowers.

I'm whispering near her ear,
afraid to disturb.
They've just got her quiet,
they tell me.

No reaction.
Not a muscle flutters.
Nothing.
I watch her with daughter-eyes.

Today she's not so beautiful,
mouth open,
bitter,
frown lines on her forehead.

Where do you go, Mama?
Are you frightened?
Are you furious?
Do you ever think of me?

9. Pleasing

The nurse pushes her down the hall
to where I stand by reception.
Here's your daughter, she says,
and I say, *Hi Mama*,
and she smiles,
and she says, *Hi dear*,
and takes my hand,
and I am stunned.

She knows me.
She touches me.
She calls me by her special name.
Dear means that I please her,
that she's happy,
that she loves me,
that I'm good!

I am sixty-four years old.

10. Thankless

Just when I think that I have run the gamut
of available hell, there is more. After yesterday's
yelling at the nurses, clawing at my face —
the elevator stops, the doors open, there she is
in front of me. Dead.

They wouldn't let her die in the hall ...

A gate inside my head
clangs shut. I am dizzy, spinning,
air thick with grey-green nausea.
There she is in her wheelchair,
head tipped back, mouth frozen open,
parchment skin colourless.
No sign of life. My breathing stops.
The air is buzzing. Everything dark.

Do something ...

I move to her,
hear the high-pitched falter of my child voice,
Mama, are you there?

I hold her wrist,
blood stirs beneath my fingers.
She chokes on air, murmurs in her sleep — alive.

I hate her for dying, I hate her for living — .
There is no place of comfort for this
thankless guilty child.

11. Milestone

My birthday, sixty-five. They say it's just
a number, but it isn't. It scares me, this descent
to senior status. They'll give me money just
because I'm old. Am I useless now, in need of
handouts? Will my health fail soon, my mind?

I take a chance, go to see my mother.
She sits in her wheelchair, skeletal and absent,
feet propped up, mouth working constantly.
No sound. I've learned to read her lips. She's tired.

Her eyes close. I tell her proudly
her grandson is teaching in Toronto.
Still she won't look at me.
"That lazy bum — he always liked to sit down
on his ass! Teachers — zero zero zero!"
Even in dementia, she knows how to strike.

Defeated, I can't tell her it's my birthday.
Leave it alone. I lose the battle with
my reddening eyes, weep in silence,
long to lay my head down on her shoulder,
feel her soft cool hand against my cheek.
Tell her I'm old. Have her fix it.

12. Ad Lib

Sweet kisses today and gentle pats over
my face, the way a baby does with her mother.
She's happy to see whoever she thinks I am.
*Did you know my mother, Lillie-Anne? There's
a hyphen.* She smiles, delighted with herself,
then corrects. *No hyphen. Lilianne. She was your
favourite grandma.* So she knows me. Don't blow it.

I tell her I remember; hope a story may emerge.
But she asks about the weather, and my older son,
and something new, a mystery man, black,
with whom she thinks I share my home.
Her greatest fear was that I'd run away with
someone on my *list of ethnic boyfriends*.

She's off again, smiling. Tells me her father was
transported down the other day — taken from his
heavenly home. A tall white angel pushed him
in a wheelchair. He came to see her acting
in a play, without a script. She had to make it up —
an ad lib play! Holds my hand in hers, tells me
he loved her in it. *Clapped and clapped!* she says.

I don't know where her brain goes
but today there is a lightness.
She needs to see her daddy
and she simply serves him up.
She needs to love her daughter,
and she smiles and pats my face.
She wants to bless us all, and she does.
I hope she dies like this.

13. Camp Nana

Each on a side of her bed
we watch my mother drag for air,
wave away food and fluids, enunciate
in sepulchral tones to the nurses
"I – will – ask" — the last words I'll hear her say.

Day melts into evening into night;
there are no chairs and we set up
"Camp Nana" on the floor in the corner.
We have thought to bring coffee,
sandwiches, fruit for the vigil.
The night nurse brings us blankets.

We listen to the rasping breath,
tuck in her bedding all around, as we did
for our children when they were small.
We doze a little — panicked awake, once,
by the supervisor's flashlight —
then back to listening in the dark,
the everlasting open-mouthed struggle
lending structure to the night.

So many hours, so many breaths.

We're into another day
before the rhythm falters.
I hear it, I lean in —
I've got you, Mama, it's okay,
I'm holding you. A choke, a gasp,
and gently she is gone.

14. Ring

April 10, 1937: a ceremony at home
during the Great Depression,
she in her good blue dress,
no wedding gown, no big jewel,
just the sweet white gold ring
with its seven tiny diamond chips —
I used to count them, as a child,
sitting in her lap: none missing.
How I loved that ring!
Today I slip it from her finger,
put it in my pocket.

> *I see her now, kneeling in the earth.*
> *She's peering over her glasses*
> *at three tiny crocus cups.*
> *She turns to me, beaming.*
> *Just look at these little miracles,*
> *she says.*

15. The World Again
August 2005, Salmon River

By the bank I find a dragonfly
sunning in the slow summer breeze,
the air thick with cicadas'
high persistent droning.

Needle body,
eyes alert for business —
glass-transparent wings
glinting in the sun

this late August afternoon
shining river-blue,
this fifteenth day of
motherlessness.

Tiny Suns

Up through the canopy of old-growth oaks
and a gasp of September blue,
beyond the limits of vision, in my mind's eye
the rosy bubble of N11 Nebula,
deep in the universe's womb,
nurseries of baby stars astonishing in their brightness.

In the nest where my grandchild lives,
feet propped up against the rich red wall
of her mother's belly, she is lulled
by measured cadences of maternal heartbeat —
resting, sustained, content
to float and dream.

Those tiny suns, infants of N11, do they too bask,
soothed by rhythms of the Mother's deep
humming? Is there nurture in fire and dust,
the hot swirling winds?

Idyll

A dark emerald of moss shares the cliff face
with black lichen, patchy and tenacious. I fall
five hundred miles and sixty years into a memory:
scaling the High Rock with my mother
in her wide-legged shorts, my brother
catching grasshoppers, hands stained with "spit."

We reach for the top, legs juniper-scratched,
bruised from misjudging jumping distance.
High summer on the Shield — red sumac, goldenrod.
My brother upturns clumps of earth,
revealing colonies of ants, pale slugs,
carapaced beetles scurrying and confused.

The prize — ah, the prize is always the view: blue lake,
wooden boat, rented cabin. We wave and wave
at nobody, bounce echoes off the cliffs.
Perched on boulders we open knapsacks —
bologna sandwiches with ketchup, canteens
of tinny lukewarm water, fresh-picked blueberries.

At night we sleep on homemade bunks: a closet
of a bedroom, one log wall, one beaverboard, tiny
hooked window. Mushrooms push at floorboards, mice
squeeze impossibly through chinking. Always the smell
of coal oil and cigarettes from the other room,
music from the portable radio. Mosquitoes.

Nocturne

If we were really good,
if our mother said we had been,
we were treated to some Chopin
on the old used player
our dad brought home one day,
some scratched LPs thrown in unheard.

Bath, bed, and finally the piano,
sparkly rivulets floating us down
through the spun wool of consciousness
Tim and I tucked safely in —
faded flannel sheets,
blue checkered quilts.

Chopin — not my rigid
daytime father's style at all,

the longing in each pearly note,
the undertone of deep accepting sadness
conspiring with him to carry us
to safe untroubled sleep.
He was magical, this nighttime papa,
playing us Chopin in our beds.

Still

1.

I hold him, still, from time to time,
in the cup of my hands,
glance inside
at his small blue flame.
Fragile. No heat.

In the end, I just stopped trying.
Forgot, God help me
that he couldn't possibly
stay here
in the blizzard
of his life.

Turned away,
even as I swore
on our hot close blood
on his bottomless fear,

to keep his hand in mine.

2.

He will always be a kid:
a tall tender boy,
my brother who shot himself
with one crack of our father's gun.

At the funeral, consolations.
It was no one's fault, the dark red pain,
the rifle. Not our fault, they said.
No one's fault. As if they knew.

3.

He walked down the front steps
of my home, turned,
smiled,

promised I didn't have to worry now,
promised he'd be okay.
Told me to be happy,
happy with your new guy.

His last words.

Well-intentioned, he would argue.
Did he really think
the surprise would *spare* me?
Furious, I spit the word.

But mostly,
most of the time
underneath my skin,
I'm broken still.

4.

What he missed —

Kent State
Woodstock
Tiananmen Square

                    our mother growing old
                    closing the heart-door.
                    When she was dying
                    she never spoke his name

smashing the Berlin Wall
the Gulf War
Nine/Eleven

Our father
who took forever
to drink himself to death
eighteen years of sleepless
booze-soaked moaning
midnight walking

Desert Storm
gay marriage
Arab Spring

My sons, our lives, our future

suicide by bomb

Year End 2007

There, violence laid open — blazing, bedlam, blood — carnage
    in Rawalpindi.
Benazir. The hopeless hope of her.

Stunned reporters dodge rage-fuelled bombs, transport us to
    ravaged shops,
howling mothers, dead children.

Here on our road the snow melts, freezes, mud-spattered. The
    dog too, in and out of jagged
ditches, sluggish slime

where drowned oak leaves cling to rusted bottle caps — one
    newly broken pine bough,
silvergreen, an unexpected balm.

Our temporary neighbours in these woods are packing,
    focused, trying to beat the coming storm,
up and down the hill,

planning New Year's Day with families back home. Trudging
    to vans festooned with skis and
winter toys. Blue smoke wisps

from the chimney, fairy lights still frame the front door. We
    shout Happy New Year, wave until
they disappear.

From the television later, a choir. *Panis Angelicus*. Sweet boy
    voices surrounding us. Feeding us
small starved scraps of peace.

Mirage, Whitefish Lake

I'm staring out the window at the lake
where images of bright striped
toques appear, out on the ice, which
snaps and cracks like thunder —
big boots, long legs, frozen bursts
of breath. Seeing my sons so clearly
from yesterday, I hold on to my hope
that the universe itself can conjure
miracles of ocular remembering,
visions of those souls who can't return.

Another Ending

I'm living by the lake now. Just your cup of tea.
The bay is perfect for a boat, like the one you built
in our garage when I was still a kid.
Remember how the neighbours came to watch you
after supper, turn to one another, laughing —
He'll never wrap it up.

You could build a log house like we did
when Tim was ten. You taught him, shy and anxious,
to haul huge logs, hammer spikes, work like a man.
My job was finding *chuckies*, little stones
we stuffed into the cracks of the fireplace
built from rocks you'd been collecting forever.

I have grandkids who would play with you, love the tunes
you used to sing — *The Russian Lullaby*, the sad, sad
        Hobo Song
and then, when we were drifting off, *Goldmine in the Sky*.
You could spin your tales about the Great Depression,
selling French newspapers on the streets of Montreal,
cooking up potatoes thirty ways.

How I long to see you with the bandy legs your Glasgow pappy
handed down, dancing wild and laughing in the hallway,
the way you were before the pain, the never-ending drink,
the strangled tears. We could lift our faces,
shuffle around a bit.
Forgive.

Under Siege

Closed up in her narrow room,
single cot, homemade dresser,
fraying wall of beaver board,
she is defended by a book tower
from the library in town —
Mazo de la Roche, Nancy Drew,
Lucy Maud and her intrepid Anne.
It is 1950 and she is ten.

There is rain, the flutter
of red and white gingham
at the small open window,
the room's sole decoration
a painted clay figure,
the hunkering "squaw"
she won at the Foley Fall Fair.

Her brother loves this camp,
off playing Tarzan with his friends
while she reads, head down,
trying not to wait, trying to breathe without
the dread creeping to where she thinks
her heart is. Heart, muscles, lungs,
all under siege.

A piece of her brain listens
unbidden, draws her in,
hunches her shoulders up to her ears,
makes her head hurt. She knows
petitioning God, *Please Jesus*, is useless.
The cupboard door will always creak,
gin will be poured, her father will fall into it.
And nobody, ever, will stop pretending.

Night Window

A candle gutters on the scarred wooden table.
Through the open window
night breezes quicken,

unheeded by an old man bent as if in prayer,
but not. Nor in sorrow
nor meditation.

Because she knows him, and because she is his daughter
she understands he is finished with these things;
also regret, despair, tears.

Head slumped on his chest,
his posture speaks of emptiness — mind, heart,
bottle on the floor.

She wants to call his name,
but she knows he is comfortless,
and she is dreaming him again.

Nobody Talks

Mother purrs a hello,
cools when she hears his voice

and still he calls every day at five —
"Anything you need?"

Home from work,
he kisses her cheek

pats her bottom
tries for a hug,

never gets one.

Solitary martinis;
he tells the clamouring kids to go and play —
they do, afraid to argue.

Her voice, the chill of it,
announces dinner.

The kitchen table looms,

his soup-stained tie,
wet, slack mouth,
her pursed lips,

nobody talks.

Decades on,
when he, less resolute than she,
tires of the game, and dies of it,

she weeps like a forsaken child,
cradles his well-worn cane in her arms.

Mea Culpa for My Father

The alarm went off at six.
Morning rituals —
smoker's cough, quiet groan,
up to pee.

Then down the stairs for coffee,
flick and click, familiar smell
of lighter fluid, wisp of smoke,
thundering fart.

Shower, shave,
Vitalis to his sluggish scalp,
almond-scented Jergens
to his face.

I used to hurry to the bathroom when he left,
inhale the reassurance of him.

I never told him that.

Depot Harbour, 1961

Working on the kids' ward
to earn tuition for my last year
of nursing school, I glimpsed
another world. Our small hospital served
a ghost town: Wasauksing land
on Georgian Bay, which had
(before we shouldered in
to "buy" it from them)
seen happier days.

Then, squalor: limp grey sheets
flapped listlessly on sagging lines;
dogs everywhere, not friendly;
scruffy, boisterous kids,
skin chalky from the dust.

They came to us with coughs and fevers,
broken bones, burst ear drums,
sometimes stayed for days and days,
until we could hunt down
a next-of-kin, or anyone at all
to fetch them home
when they were healed.

We fed them, found them giggling,
hiding in the laundry baskets, losing
bandages off fixed-up body parts,
making us laugh while we deplored the
"irresponsible parents" we could not find.

Noah stayed for weeks, our little helper,
our seemingly abandoned boy with black star-eyes,

a rascal's grin, brown velvet skin,
a fat gauze dressing on his runny ear.

He never worried — understood
without a doubt his dad would come
to take him home

> *when traps are set*
> *when fish are caught*
> *and wrapped in leaves*
> *to keep them fresh until*
> *he smokes them.*

What's Been and Lost

1. Epigraph

A cold October in the marsh —
angel-hair milkweed wisps,
black rusted bracken,
lambswool on cattails.

Fog and shadow
play tricks on vision.
So easily the water
gives itself to ice.

2. Knowing

Again she feels the whisper of his beard
against her cheek,
hears his laugh. It's been
a long time.
She turns to him in bed,
eager, her heart
unfurling — and wakes to remember.

Her old ginger cat rests
against her face.
Nose to nose in the thick dark
they absorb the moment,
sink together back to sleep.

3. The Body Remembers

Suffused with autumn,
my body remembers
hearing your ragged breathing
claw at the liquor-soaked air.
Sees your bloody mouth
in the scarlet of the maples.
Feels the gun-metal cold
of mid-October.

There was cold rain at your funeral.

Today the rain comes hard
in these tattered woods,
wind rages, whips my hair,
threatens my heartbeat
with the smell of your dying.

4. Running Up the Back Stairs

Faded plaid shirt,
ripped sleeves,
worn like a vest
over everything.

Worn out work boots,
shapeless jeans,
sawdust in his beard.

A huge roaring giant,
he loved music,
Christmas,
hockey.

He brought me
a silver kitten once.

Paul,
running up the back stairs
laughing.

5. No Door

After his father dies
brutally
by his own hand
my elder son
seventeen
goes to bed for months
and won't get up
or talk to us
except to tell his brother
what everybody says —
you will have to
help your mother
now your dad has gone.

His brother, twelve,
terrified of everything
makes dinners
and stays in his room
drawing pictures
in the night, dreaming
that his dad returns
by airplane
to convince his boy
to fly with him to a
thousand-storied
dwelling in the sky

He never cries.

I want to comfort them,
but I never find the door
much less the key —

What can you say
when their father
shoots a hole
into his lovely head
and lives
for endless days
unconscious
in a hospital room

then dies
alone
while we at home
hole up
like wounded beasts?

6. Legacy

You loved our sons
without restraint —
they made you laugh
until tears brimmed.

You teased, called them
buddy, bud, budinski
They loved you back with
all their young boy hearts.

So who do you think you are
teaching them love
doesn't count?

7. Dissolving

At Union Station
I disembark into
familiar Toronto damp.
Tears well unexpectedly,
pain twisting hard
under my left rib.

From the taxi window
I see you everywhere —
shade in Riverdale,
baseball diamond ghost,
departed gourmand of
Danforth Avenue kitchens.

I'm afraid that you
will vanish soon —
shape dissolving, face fading.
Gone the perfect teeth,
curly beard, black hair
shining in the sun.

My drowned eyes
will lose you then,
exactly as these traitor ears
misplaced your loving laugh.

8. Twenty Years After

I broke into the old place
where I found you dying
in your upstairs lair among the
fishing rods, the punching bag,
the guns — the goddam guns.

No one lives there now,
but decades of ravaging
by the derelicts who bought
our suicide house for nothing
nearly did me in.

There is no human language for
the wet, grey stench clinging
to our bedroom. Brimming ashtrays,
broken bottles, wadded tissues.

It was the boys' rooms, small,
dank, the yellowed scraps of
wallpaper, that gutted me.

My god, that childhood wallpaper —
those silver airplanes,
those friendly bears.

9. Found

I still look for you,
as if I could find you in the garden,
see you standing by the lake,
as if that knock at my door
could be you.

This morning our granddaughter,
the little one you never met,
sits on the floor
playing peek-a-boo with me.

She laughs, this girl,
head thrown back,
mouth wide open
to drink in her delight.

Straight from her belly, she laughs
and laughs. And here you are.

Soft Shoe

1. Requiem

Cure is not a word in her current
cancer lexicon. Remission, once in, is out,
the dreamed Baltic cruise left unplanned.
It's not that I'm afraid of dying
she says this afternoon.
I just don't want to — I want to see it
all unfold — you know? She falters,
laughs, apologetic — she hadn't
meant to bring it up. But there it is.
Her beloved Mozart, the Requiem,
playing in her head. Her leaving begun.

2. Echo

"My cancer has come back."

I plant lettuce, zucchini, peas

    She said it plain as though it were
    swallows and Capistrano

tuck carrot specks into black earth

    just a crumb of ordinary information

transplant peonies into the sun

    It has come back

sow seeds for poppies, wildflowers

    reappeared, returned

feed and water them

    Untended

watch pale green beans unfurl, seed casings opening

    seeds carried by blood
    settling in, waiting to bloom

3. Misplaced

The steroid dose is through the roof.
She takes it — flies on dexamethasone,
then crashes. This woman who takes
refuge in my heart, calls from day to day
to tell me that she finds herself a little left
of centre. *Don't come*
is in her voice.

She's hiding underneath
her duvet, weeping like a child, not
knowing how to stop, ashamed
to be among the frightened and the lost.
No pull-yourself-together, no
ramrod spine. Betrayed by tears,
her Englishness has fled.

Weeks later they tell her it's the steroids,
forgot to mention it before: depression
a side effect.

Freed from hidden terrors,
façade restored,
she smiles.

4. Ragged with Holes

Nobody can get the bacon
right, and I am fretting,
needing to satisfy your end-of-life
cravings the minute they surface.
At last, a butcher in the village
produces a tender centre-cut,
lean and salty, rolled in
perfect grainy peameal.

I roast it in fresh
orange juice and ginger beer
exactly as my mother taught me.
A razored slice
with half a scrambled
nest-born
organic egg
precisely centred
on a lightly toasted
near-transparent slice
of your best Italian bread.

You pronounce it orgasmic.
Probably my last one, you grin,
and hand me my birthday bag,
the one we've traded gifts in
for as long as we've been friends,
ragged with holes now, taped together.
The one you said you couldn't find
this year. Then did.

5. Midwinter

The road is frozen steel;
the lake too,
with whorls of glass
and snow engraved by
yesterday's scouring wind —
raw, relentless,
all but obscuring
a cold distant sun.

There are no colours
here, no breath
but mine and the dog's.
She eyes me from vision's edge,
nervous in the planet's
vast white silence.
A dark thrust
of granite looms.
A sudden crow.

I look for you —
notice far off tracks,
rabbit, fox, coyote,
the scarlet slash
of a kill. Life. Then not.
I remember holding you
the day you died —
you, flinging your arm
across your forehead,
so tired of the waiting.

6. Indelible

That image of you
walking in front of me
down the short hall
from the kitchen to
the bed where you lived then —
clutching a duo of forks and knives,
decked out in my soft pajama T-shirt
and a pair of pristine underpants,
loose enough to protect your tender skin,
tight enough to hold up dressings
and tubes.

Nodding your small bald head,
under your breath a tune
about long shaky shanks,
you shuffle a brilliant little soft shoe,
although your feet are bare
and white against the dark wood floor.

Sixtieth Anniversary

Pouched pale eyes — that watery gaze
never coming to rest, avoiding contact.
Her illness. His grief.

Everyone trying to boost his spirits. Congratulations,
jokes. Not what he wants. He casts around,
catches my eye, moves as if his life hangs upon it.

Never a one to spill words, he holds me
with bewildered sorrow, senses I will hear him out
while we watch his wife, bent double,

forever unable to see the sky,
like a black-shrouded crone in an old Greek movie.
Their daughter helps her up the stairs

and I want to run to them, ease the painful
snails' crawl. But I stay.
She used to run the business, you know —

the ordering, the books, a few difficult customers.
So much smarter than me. I didn't tell her enough
back then but I tell her now.

The arthritis came so sudden — a few aches and pains, then
one day nothing moves. She lies in bed. Touch her wrong,
she whimpers. You know how a pup sounds. Like that.

All our lives. The kids, the business, never imagining
old age would come at all, leastways not like this,
so cruel, so pitiful.

He searches my face, squeezes my arm.
Nice to see you after all these years.

Unlocked

Ice melts on the lake
and blackbirds scream.

In the woods
pale beginnings —
small shy petals
trembling.

Molly and Her Man

Widowed, come together late,
they are partners — their kids
grateful to miss the burden
of their old age for a while.

Friendly, chatty, but careful,
wary of past errors,
lacerating wars, tender scars.
Their bodies fit together

if not often, nicely enough
to keep them in the same big bed,
affectionate and easy. But
Molly wishes for a little more

romance, a small display of feeling.
Just a smidge, she thinks. Then,
slowly as the coming of spring, she
senses a tiniest unfurling, hears

her name, a light caress.
You say my name, she says.
It's nice. You name me more.
He looks at her, surprised.
Ah, Moll, he says. I love you more.

To Sleep

The woods on a May evening, new-green
and gold, the lake still as smoked glass.

Streams of fire flood the sky, sharing
the lake's reflection with oak and evergreen.

Blackbirds call themselves to sleep.

The tiny wren is already in her house —
she's early to rise, that little yakker.

Soon the sun will make its way
behind the house, behind the trees,

then disappear, concealing all —

bright oriole, goldfinch, thrush — wrapping us
in the velvet sound of owl.

Moon. Stars.

Here and Now

Sometimes I wonder —
when the shocking thrill
of our widowed
old age loving
surrenders its edge,
will I still
embrace it?

Or did I simply
snap you up
to not be solitary
any more,
to not discuss
my every thought
with fading ghosts
and aging orange cats.

This morning
you went out.
And now
the kitchen sun
illuminates
the age spots
on my hand,
your empty coffee cup,
the wrecked old shirt
you wear to cut the grass
draped on the chair across from mine.

Well Bred

Explosion of wings!
In the underbrush, we stop,
the young dog and I.
She looks at me —
what's this —
It's a partridge, I say.
Just a partridge.

We stand on the side of the road,
watch the bird walk quietly, carefully,
into the autumn woods,
brown into brown.

Well, I say to my dog
they sure bred the hunter out of you!
She sits in front of me,
lifts her beautiful head to the sky,
looks at me upside down,
grins like a wolf.

The Black Wolf Hotel

1. A Quaint Pub

Uprooting themselves from
a seething metropolis
they come seeking safety for their kids,
and something they can do
together.

They picture a bucolic paradise —
organic food from nearby farms,
a quaint pub, a jolly rumpus
with music, darts,
solid country folk.

She'll cook
do the books
help out on weekend nights
when they can find a sitter.

He'll run the pub
chat with customers (he's good at this)
keep the old place looking good.

But soon enough she learns to deep-fry
everything — no one but the kids
will eat her pilafs, her salads.
He drinks too much — a bar fight early on —
baseball bats, blood.

She hears it on the street —
a guy who frightens her
leaning up against her hip, his breath
liquor-hot.

I hear you bought the *Dirty Dog*,
he snickers. What are you — fucking crazy?

2. Septic Sustenance

Cool sweet melons.

Carrots, squash, pumpkin, potatoes,
every kind of bean.

They never had a garden —
a few impatiens, scarlet geraniums,
poppies they stole from the neighbours,

but never sustenance straight from the earth —
their own patch of it.

Teaching the kids about cycles and seasons,
family sweat.

She takes a photo of her ten-year-old,
shirt off, straw hat, huge grin.
Her farmer boy hoeing his rows.

They heap the hotel menu with colour and taste —
secret laughter when they catch
a plate of broccoli

just before they serve it
studded with curly green worms —
perfectly steamed.

Their own little Eden,
but too close to the septic. He clicks his pen,
that grave young health inspector.

— We ploughed it under,
sowed some old grass seed
we found in the shed.

3. A Jolly Rumpus

A down-and-out housewife,
dress torn, stumbles into the hotel,
hunted down by her husband,
stone-faced, fist at the ready.

Nobody's business,
nobody helps —

not the construction crew
hired to work at the nearby canal
shouting for drinks and hot food,

not the regulars, silently watching them paw
love-hungry local girls clutching at dreams,
abandoned with little kids,

not the bartender too busy
short-changing people
to slake his own thirst for booze.

Saturday night at the Dirty Dog,
camaraderie turning to drunken bravado,
fights breaking out like brushfires until
somebody snaps, and the mob
puts the boots to Bill Murphy's face.

— We sold them the alcohol, lifted
car keys, gave rooms
for the night. Cleaned up their
mess in the morning.
Washed the sheets.

4. Short Order Cook

Closing time come and gone, and still they sit,
nodding in liquored affability,
endlessly repetitive,
full of love with sloppy smiles.

After ten kids, still such gorgeous legs,
her husband, drunker than drunk,
slurs to the late night clientele as we
try to shoo them out.

And gorgeous they are, those legs. At sixty,
costumed for this Halloween night
in mini-skirt, six-inch heels and sheer black tights
she gestures perfectly like Carol Channing.

The men take in the sexy thigh-crossed legs,
no one sharp enough to catch her proud, shy pleasure,
years of heartache vanished in the arch of neck,
the lift of chin, elegant tilt of her cigarette.

She worked for us, short-order cooking
for the lunchtime rush, always a beer
half-hidden under the sink. She told me once,
makeup running down her face —

Ten kids, she said.
No one drank at home, you know.
I never touched a drop until I married him.

5. Handy Man

He died at thirty-eight, a stroke, long
wrap-around pompadour askew, baldness
a final shaming. The oldest of ten *plus one dead*,
pulled from school early when mum and dad
were at the bar, kids abandoned
in the truck by the hotel. We helped him
bring them in, set them by the fire,
heated up soup, turned on cartoons.
When they grew up, those kids, they broke in
and stole our food, remembering.

He called us Ma and Pa, taught our youngest
how to paint a wall when he was five. Patient
as a monk. Sweet, clever, always drunk, he never
missed a day. But booze which kept him on his feet
at work, rendered him mute and helpless every night.

His brother beat on him — his frightened sister called.
We took him home, tended to him in our spare room,
a palace to this shack boy, jammed in a bedroom
with his siblings, hauling on the blankets.
He never had a woman.
His chronic sweet befuddlement, the silly
pompadour (his only vanity) would turn them
all away. Oh Simon, they would tell him,
go away, you've pissed yourself — telltale stains
on faded jeans, impossible to miss.

Our children never noticed, took his hand
to cross the road, shared their cokes,
stopped to watch him work.
Stained fingers, false teeth at thirty.
He made us smile. He broke our hearts.

So long ago, when we were all alive.

A Farm Wife's Tale

1.

Jesus came by the other day. Tom was down milking,
and I was peeling potatoes, when I seen him
from the kitchen window tramping up the lane.
Knew him straight off, couldn't tell you why —
he didn't look one tiny little bit like that
gold-edged painting in the Holy Bible,
the one we had at Sunday School —
I remember He had long pale hair,
and Miss Pritchard surely loved Him, she was
always going on about Him, always
"our Dear Lord's eyes, shining blue with love..."
imagine me remembering that all these years!

This Jesus looked a lot like that nice doctor
who came to the farm when Tom was sick
with the sugar diabetes. Right here to the house —
imagine — we were much taken with his doctoring,
so I was well disposed to letting this poor
look-alike Jesus in the door. I still can't figure
how I knew him right away. His eyes and hair
were dark as night, his face was tanned
the color of black walnut, even in this godforsaken
cold. Looked like he didn't have a pot to piss in
(*excuse the saying, especially in a story about you, Lord*).
The sadness, maybe. How I knew him. I think so.

Well. I let him in and even remembered from the Bible
to ask if he wanted his feet washed. But he said no —
no thanks — I don't really feel like taking off my boots
if you don't mind, I'm pretty tired. He did look all done in.
He looked like he was going to cry.
Or maybe sink himself into the big brown chair
and never be able to stir his bones again.

64

So I didn't ask him about the stories
we studied so long ago — walking on water,
feeding all them people,
getting crucified, poor lad.
I didn't want to remind him.

He did take a cup of coffee with me, and two
oatmeal cookies, so quiet, sitting in the nice
warm kitchen toasting his tootsies, boots and all
(*if I'm allowed to say that about your holy self*)
beside the woodstove which was stoked up
for the potatoes. I could see he was fighting sleep
so I offered him a nap in the spare room.
But he said he had to take his leave. Said he felt
restored now — having shared this peaceful time.
He'd been so lonely on the road. He'd looked up
and seen me through the kitchen window
with my face of warmth and kindness. Imagine —
the blessing! Shared, he said. Him. And me.

2.

I'm just trying this out Jesus —

seeing as we shared — you said it, not me.

I'm asking you to see if God would let this cup

pass from our lips.

I remember that you prayed about it in that garden

when you thought you just couldn't do it —

the dying part, the getting crucified.

I know it didn't work for you because it was

part of the rules of you being here.

But Tom?

Maybe you could try.

Maybe there aren't no special rules for him.

3.

They say it helps to talk. Well.
It started with a bleeding lump,
the tiniest little lump on Tom's ankle,
just above the bone. A mole
with a lump on it. And he scratched it
to bleeding, and then it wouldn't stop.
So they done some tests, then x-rays,
then they told us melanoma.
We didn't have the foggiest idea
he would die of it. They never said.

He kept up the chores for quite a spell
until he couldn't get his air in.
They said the cancer got itself wrapped
around his breathing tube, and then it got
to pressing on his heart — started in
the ankle and ended in his heart.
Ended his heart and ended him.
My Tom. Married fifty-three years
and never slept one night apart.
Ripped away, just like that.

I'd sure like to see that Jesus now,
him and his sharing. (*Sorry for being
so cross about you. Sorry, Jesus*). Just
can't figure why he came for that visit
last October. Put his feet up. Took
coffee and cookies with me, so quiet
and sorrowful. I'm thinking maybe he knew
about Tom and just couldn't say. Anyways —
the kids are driving up tonight. Funeral tomorrow.
Fifty-three years. I never been alone.

4.

Well, God, you just couldn't pass that dying cup

to anyone else — I guess it wouldn't'a been fair,

I guess it was Tom's time to go,

and I'm thinking that you maybe just can't change that.

Or Jesus either, even if he did try, which I don't know

because he never came back.

And Jesus, if you're listening, this is bad to say

but I can't help it.

I'm pretty riled at you, and

at God too

for not being able to change the rules.

And at Tom for leaving me —

5.

Who woulda guessed it, but I seen him again.
I thought I heard the geese coming home,
and just had to take a look out the shed door.
I don't go out much since Tom passed —
seems I got no interest any more,
no strength, no happy heart.
But geese now — geese mean spring,
and I was out the door before I knew it.

And not one goose in sight — way too early — but
a body has to hope sometimes to just keep going.
I know that Tom would want me to.
Up and at 'em Mary-Ellen, he would of said.
God gave you life to live it out. So don't be wasting it.
— Well, Tom, no geese, just a bunch of noisy crows.
But they were honking, pretending, joking around
like crows do. Teasing me into getting up
and running to the door, bad knees and all.

I seen a little movement over near the barn —
it startled me some, because young Brad from down the road
was here real early to fetch the cows and do the milking.
And he left — I seen him through the window — he has school,
and his own chores to do before the bus comes.
There should of been nobody near, and my heart took
to pounding till I saw that it was Jesus. Come again.
I had a sudden notion that he made them crows honk
to get me out the door. Made me laugh, I don't know why.

Then laughing made me cry — no Tom to share it.
And there was Jesus watching. And I wasn't scared at all,
same as that other day he came. He didn't talk this time,

just leaned against the barn door, quiet, kind of serious,
looking in my eyes. And I could see he knew about my pain.
He kind of took my pain all calm, and I could tell
he knew it. Knew my pain for Tom.
So I gave it to him. We shared it.
And then he left — didn't disappear or rise up
to heaven like in the movies or the Bible,
just straightened up and walked back down the lane.
Didn't wave or turn around at all.

Sometimes I wonder why he comes to me like this?
Seems like he might have better things to do.
But you know, it helped to give it over.
The awful hurt, I mean, and how mad I am at Tom
and how mad I am at God. And the kids who never call.
Or come by hardly ever.

Autumn with Birds

A quiet day on the lake
except for the sound of someone
chopping wood. Leaves are down
or ready to fall — waiting for signals.
Wisps of sadness hover.

The sky is that rare shade of blue
you can feel in your chest.
No clouds. A crisp chill niggles —
get out the sweaters and boots,
pull up the boats, take the air conditioner
out of the bedroom window.

Up here late autumn begets
a certain blindness to beauty.
Folks with heads down
going about their chores —
putting stripped gardens to bed,
canning and freezing, tending steaming kettles.
Rituals learned in childhood.

Suddenly, a swirling cloud
darkens the sky, filling the air
with a jungle of bird call.
They always arrive in a burst, raucously:
thousands of black birds perch
on the old growth maples and oaks
pouring their music down,
enveloping us in resounding chatter.

They set the trees to a furious flutter,
then rise as one, ribboning the sky,
opening our faces,
our hidden places.

Like Water

When they are seventeen he takes her to a place
where the Shield surrounds, and Kelly's Creek
pinches to a rivulet, tadpoles flashing through
sunken moss, sunshine winking on puddles like
an eyelid when the light is too brilliant to face.

They lie together in the shallows, these childhood friends,
unschooled in passion, drawn in by the shimmer of tiny
minnows and the ripe scent of slow slippery pools. Sweet
easy kisses, hesitant touchings, then a melting so warm,
so new, their laughter wells up in astonishment.

A fifty year old memory, rising from beneath a
guarded heart, unseemly in its longing, as vibrant
as if yesterday — me so young and careless
shaking love out of my hair like water.

Rachmaninoff

Her father, excessive and misguided
as he often is, calls his favorite composer
Rocky Baby, speaking what he thinks is
her lingo, determined to wean his girl
from her cacophony of rock and roll.

She humours him, listens, falls in love.
She is eighteen, full of passion and despair,
caught up in the grandeur, beauty, grief.
It takes her breath,
it makes her weep.

Later, at thirty, besotted with her babies,
she turns to Haydn. At forty, filled
with shifts and yearning — Beethoven.
Mozart and Schumann fill her fifties
and sixties with a purity
otherwise long gone.

Seventy is Bach, only Bach,
staying dark fears.
But sometimes — in a thunder night
of waves on rocks, or crouching small
inside a lonely midnight silence,
Bach cannot contain her.

She lets them come then —
Rachmaninoff in full flight
wide open, soaring.
Her father, laughing,
spinning her round the kitchen,
roaring out the music.

Leaf

Black branch against sky — oak, stubborn leaves
always last to depart, unwilling to shrivel and fall.
She watches the new day rise with the sun,
has been up for hours with the pain in her hip,
floating, avoiding deep thinking,

this grey-haired girl kidnapped by time.

She forgets if she took her pills, fed the cats, really lost
her slippers. Walks invisible on the streets, loses herself
in the wash of indifference, loses her balance,
loses her nerve. She calms the clunk of her
double-crossed heart for fear of the big attack,

nightmares of nursing home, walkers and wheelchairs,
caregivers calling her honey. She thinks of her mother,
weeps with the shame of not having understood.
She misses the grandkids, pining to hold them,
knowing as everyone says, they have lives
of their own. As she has had hers.

And dammit, still does.

Unacknowledged Messages from the Real World in Her Seventy-First Year

My sons insist on cooking Christmas dinner
in my house.

I sport food stains on my shirt,
brown spots, large and lumpy on my face,

my toes grow curiously crooked,
and the toilet seat appears to be too low.

A new red cane, *my stick*, I say, hangs close
beside my father's, his made of sturdy oak.

In the hospital, frightened, crying,
sure that the waves of pain must mean bad news,
embarrassed by my childish display,
I hear a voice —

*a seventy-year-old woman
presenting with abdominal discomfort.*

Pulling myself together,
I offer to let her go ahead of me.

Blue Mittens

Today a young man with a sweet smile
offers his blue-mittened hand, and I,
stumbling on icy sidewalks,

                reach

instinctively, gratefully, but with jerky
awkwardness, rendered shy
by my faith in him.

Whatever the reason —
parental teaching, his open heart,
the frightening frailty of his own loved gran,

it seems he cannot pass me by.

Little Pieces

1.

He is three.
An uncle, soon to be wed,
asks him to be ring bearer,
his big sister, flower girl.
He cries, wants to be *flower boy*,
but they say he can't.

He is coached to smithereens
with the bride's small nephew,
ring bearer number two. He knows
he must not run, skip, or hop,
he must not pick his nose,
he must walk v-e-r-y s-l-o-w-l-y.

And he does. R.B. number two runs
down to his mummy, but my guy, my grandboy,
holds his own, focused and sombre —
stuns with his measured pace.
I step into the photo they send me,
chest aching to hold that little body.

2.

Grandma! He needs to show me
his tree house, sets off through the garden
and the field, strong little legs
pumping, arms keeping up the rhythm.

I trail behind, and noticing,
he runs back, wants me to zip along beside him.
I tell him I am getting old,
not a runnable grandma now.

But Grandma — he is all concern,
brown eyes (his) on brown eyes (mine),
you should have said.
I can go slowly too!

3.

He is interested in the idea of growing old.
Also of dying.
We talk about it sometimes
and I wonder at his wonder.
Your Lily-dog got old and died, right?
Sometimes people get very sick and die, right?
Like Grandpa Paul.
Like Jordie-dog will because she's old.

He is heading from the car
to the front door.
Follow me, he says.
Then — Grandma, when you die
and we are all still alive,
we will remember you so much.
We will have lots of pictures of you in our house.
I tell him thank you.

Company

After they go home
something not quite ghostly,
but with a certain barely-out-of-sight presence,
arrives in the small new house where I live alone;
something of them, my sons,

as though they are here in the next room,
just beyond,
powerfully perceived
in some mysterious part of me
hitherto unknown.

I glance quickly, secretly; talking to them,
trying to catch the shape of their bodies in the old
brown chair, or sitting at the table in the kitchen.
I startle and look, close the bedroom door
while I undress for bed.

This morning I wake, know my house is empty now.
But both the lightness and the heft of them
lingers, pillowing my head, warming me.
And in this unfamiliar and often lonely place,
I understand that I am known.

Notes

"Giacometti's Girl": Alberto Giacometti (1901–1966) was a Swiss painter and sculptor, famous for his attenuated figures in bronze. He made many paintings of a young woman named Carolyn, subject of the print described in this poem.

"Beppe Speaks": The former kingdom of Friesland is now a province in the north of Holland. *Beppe* is Grandma in Frisian; *tantes* and *omkes* are aunts and uncles; *kinderen* are children; *Onze Vader* is the Lord's Prayer.

"Oxford Street": The italicized Yiddish words (mostly adopted from Hebrew) became part of immigrant English, often used with English plurals and suffixes.

> *mezuzah*: encased minitature scroll of scriptural verses, affixed to the doorframe of a Jewish home
>
> *meshugener*: crazy person, nitwit
>
> *shochet*: ritual slaughterer for kosher meat trade
>
> *minyan*: quorum of ten men for public prayer
>
> *daven*: to recite Jewish prayers
>
> *shul*: synagogue

"Year End 2007": Benazir Bhutto, first woman to head a democratic government in a Muslim majority nation, served as Prime Minister of Pakistan from 1988 to 1990 and 1993 to 1996. A liberal and a secularist, she was assassinated on December 27, 2007 at the age of 54.

"Soft Shoe," 2. Echo: Swallows return each spring in large numbers to nest at the Mission of San Juan Capistrano in Orange County, California.

Acknowledgements

Some of the poems from "Without a Script" appeared in variant forms under the title "Poems for my Lost Mother" in *Kingston Poets' Gallery*, edited by Elizabeth Greene for Artful Codger Press. "The World Again" appeared in *The Salmon River Watershed*, edited by Milly Ristvelt for Friends of the Salmon River. An earlier, shorter version of "A Farm Wife's Tale" appeared in CV2 under the title "Giving Over." The New Quarterly published "Like Water," "Depot Harbour," "Giacometti's Girl," "Beppe Speaks," "Remembrance Day," "Molly and Her Man," and "The Cure." Thank you to the editors of these publications.

I would like to acknowledge the generous people without whom this book would not exist, beginning with the late Joanne Page for her early attention to my poems. I benefitted from workshops with Maury Breslow, Robyn Sarah in the Icehouse in Fredericton, Lorna Crozier and Patrick Lane at Wintergreen Studios, and from the input of other gifted poet-editors who read my manuscript in earlier incarnations: Mary Cameron, Craig Howes, Maureen Hynes, Maureen Harris and Laurie D. Graham. Heartfelt thanks to my poetry family, Callie, Elaine, Leslie, Marguerite, Nathalie and Ruth, for listening closely and commenting honestly.

How does one thank a perfect editor? Robyn Sarah, mentor, friend, best of the best, has been beside me all the way. Her insight, direction, her spooky ability to carve a jewel from a plethora of unnecessary words, her dedication to the fine tuning, her vision, generosity, and consummate skill hold me in wonder, in gratitude, in awe. Thank you, my friend. It has been magical.

All love to my family — you appear in my poems and reside always in my heart.

As a longtime resident of Kingston, Ontario, at a moment when Canada is redressing past wrongs, the author would like to make mention of the original inhabitants of the land on which that city is located. To acknowledge this traditional territory of the Anishinaabe and Haudenosaunee nations is to recognize their long history, and the territory's significance for the Indigenous peoples who lived, and continue to live, upon it.

About the Author

Sandra Davies is a retired palliative care nurse who grew up in Toronto and has been writing poetry since childhood. She graduated from the University of Toronto with a Bachelor of Science in nursing, and for the next forty years practised nursing in Toronto, India (Madya Pradesh), and Kingston, her home since 1989. Since retiring she has participated in creative writing workshops and had poems appear in literary magazines and anthologies; *Giacometti's Girl* is her first book. She has two adult sons and five beloved grandchildren.

We acknowledge the sacred land on which Cormorant Books operates. It has been a site of human activity for 15,000 years. This land is the territory of the Huron-Wendat and Petun First Nations, the Seneca, and most recently, the Mississaugas of the Credit River. The territory was the subject of the Dish With One Spoon Wampum Belt Covenant, an agreement between the Iroquois Confederacy and Confederacy of the Ojibway and allied nations to peaceably share and steward the resources around the Great Lakes. Today, the meeting place of Toronto is still home to many Indigenous people from across Turtle Island. We are grateful to have the opportunity to work in the community, on this territory.

We are also mindful of broken covenants and the need to strive to make right with all our relations.